BUCKET CASH FLOW

Even profit making companies can go bust with poor cash flow

Don't let it happen to you

PRASHANT NARANG

notionpress
.com

INDIA · SINGAPORE · MALAYSIA

Notion Press

Old No. 38, New No. 6
McNichols Road, Chetpet
Chennai - 600 031

First Published by Notion Press 2019
Copyright © Prashant Narang 2019
All Rights Reserved.

ISBN 978-1-68466-759-8

CONTENTS

ABOUT THE AUTHOR

Prashant Narang is a practising chartered accountant with almost two decades of experience in providing services in the fields of consulting, audit, accounting and taxation.

He has been providing services to various small and medium businesses and has fair exposure to the challenges faced by them in managing their business' finances.

He has helped various clients set up proper and effective accounting systems which provide them accurate, relevant and timely reports. This has majorly benefited the clients as they were empowered to take business decisions leading to higher profitability and smoother cash flows.

He also conducts various workshops wherein he trains business owners and their teams on the relevance of effective financial management. In these workshops, he shares methods, tools and processes which are easy to implement and which give results to business owners instantly.

In this book, he has explained the most important tool, i.e. the four bucket cash flow statement.

He is extremely committed to enhance the financial well-being of business owners through his writings, training and quality services.

He is an avid reader, an active networker and also runs a paediatric cancer initiative with his friends. He considers his ability to empathise with others as his greatest strength.

AUTHOR'S NOTE

All business owners aspire to make it big in their respective businesses. However, very few are able to achieve what they aim for. There are multiple challenges which business owners face in their path to growth. However, one common hurdle that I noticed as a consultant was the lack of good financial management of businesses.

Most of the business owners I have interacted with in the last two decades seem to have good technical knowledge about the product or the service they offer. But, when it comes to the art of managing money, they are more or less dependent on others, or that aspect of their business is totally ignored. As a result, they have to handle frequent spells of shortage of funds and maybe a loss of multiple opportunities also. A business which is properly managed financially will never go through such tough tests of the business owner's ability to arrange funds every now and then.

I have always had two types of clients - one with good financial management skills and the other who are barely managing their businesses by keeping a track of the amounts receivable or payable by them at any point in time. The former always seem to be in control of themselves and their business. Their talk clearly reflects that they consciously keep in mind the financial impact of all their actions. These businessmen exactly know what particular challenge they are facing and what they have to do to overcome that. On the other hand, the business owners who don't bother too much about the financial management of their businesses seem to be overwhelmed all the time and are worried about the challenges of running their business.

In my opinion, the business owners should never lose sight of the financial position of their companies, especially, the cash flows. I have written this book keeping in mind the owners of small and medium-sized businesses who generally shy away from this aspect, i.e. proper financial management.

The book has been written in very easy language so that it can be understood by anyone, that it is not difficult to prepare a cash flow statement and monitor the cash flows of a business. Also, one will understand the relevance of categorising the cash flows in various buckets, and then analysing them to identify the relevant action points which need to be taken by the business owner in order to keep their organisation in good financial condition.

Prashant Narang

THE EVER ELUSIVE CASH

What does the business owner need the most to run a business? Obviously, it is money. It is needed from the very first day of any business. No business idea can see the light of the day without funds. No machinery can be bought, no team can be hired, no factory can be built, no office can be set up, and no showroom can be opened if one doesn't have cash. By cash, I don't mean physical currency notes; it denotes money in any form.

Once it is up and running, business owners' perpetual endeavour is to earn enough profits from their business, and they work really hard day and night to achieve it. However, even when their businesses are earning huge profits, they struggle with the availability of enough cash to sustain, to pay their vendors on time, to meet all the expenses and overheads, to honour the loan repayment instalments and even to run their own households.

They know they are earning on each sale they make, but money in hand always seems less. Where does the money go after all? Very few dig down deep and try to find out why is it so that after year on year with growth in sales and profits, the business keeps struggling with liquidity. They certainly have an overall understanding of their business, but what do they actually do, both at macro and micro levels, to address this liquidity problem. Maybe, nothing more is done but the juggling and managing of liabilities so that they are able to keep the boat in the waters; one liability traded for another.

How many of us would have seen businesses which were doing just fine, suddenly going bust? Actually, they don't suddenly crash. They prepare themselves over the years for this suicide. It is like slowly poisoning themselves, and it is only then that people realise the amount of poison that was inside the body.

I didn't want to start this book on such a horrifying note, but I wanted to shake you up a little so that you look into your business and ensure that it is not in the same race of poisoning itself to death.

If you are facing challenges on the liquidity front, read this book not only from the perspective of understanding what constitutes the crunch, but also understand what actions you need to take to ensure that your business doesn't crumble under the burden of unfulfilled promises to pay.

Due to lack of liquidity, one ends up paying higher interests to banks for the working capital limits and the term loans. Also, the vendors remain on the guard while dealing with the poor paymasters. They don't extend much credit or keep very high margins while dealing with such customers. Employees of such businesses always remain dissatisfied because they either get paid late perpetually or don't get appropriate appraisals at year end. The overall mood of a company, which is pressed hard for cash at all times, is generally low and less productive.

To this, the entrepreneurs heading such companies may say that it is easier said than done, and they can challenge anyone to run their company more efficiently than they are doing. Obviously, they know their company the best. They built it. It is similar to a mother who knows the best about her child. No one else can replace a mother. But, if a mother herself is ignorant to the needs of the child or is only good at taking care of one of the needs and forgets about the others, it can be really disastrous for the child. Suppose, she just takes care of the health of the child, and her focus is only on the next meal that the child is going to have but does absolutely nothing about the child's education. Would you call such a mother a good mother? Despite her ignorance, she is still the mother of the child and only she is responsible for the overall well-being and development of her child.

So, business owners can't get away with the responsibility of managing the finances of their company. If the external factors are unfavourable, they still have to manage their businesses. There is no escape. You have to know how you can monitor and capture this ever elusive cash.

The problem is not that big actually. If we get to the root cause of any business getting into trouble, we can find that it is just that the business owners don't monitor things on a timely basis, and they operate on numerous assumptions. If the management becomes a little aware of their liquidity and ensure they are on top of it at all times, they will be able to take immediate action the moment it goes haywire and not let it get worse. The problem is the lack of awareness, and more so, the willingness to be aware. People love to live in illusions than to take some action. They would look at their profit and loss account showing profits, and totally ignore the most important financial statement, i.e. the cash flow statement.

We will understand later in this book how the management of any business can easily monitor its funds on the basis of a simple cash flow statement. The **Four Bucket Cash Flow**™ **Statement,** explained later in the book, is the standard cash flow statement with a little tweak. A little in-depth analysis of this cash flow statement brings out the areas where the management or business owners should focus immediately and take action.

Another aspect which really highlights the importance of cash flows is business valuation. A very common method of valuation of a businesses is the Discounted Cash Flow Method.

That is nothing but the present value of the projected future cash flows of a company. In case a company is generating handsome cash flows, the valuation obviously is going to be higher than a company which is not expecting a great cash flow situation in the future years.

If the value of a business is calculated not based on the profits, but the cash flows it generates, you better accept the importance of keeping an eye on the cash flow statement.

CHALLENGES IN MONITORING

Though we have understood in the last chapter that monitoring of cash flows and liquidity is of utmost importance for the survival of the business, we just can't ignore the challenges faced by the management in getting accurate and reliable data. The practical experience of working with various businesses shows that there are a few common challenges faced by business owners in order to have a cash flow statement periodically.

Challenge 1
Incomplete and inaccurate Accounting Data

The root cause of not reliable and accurate data is as simple as improper accounting or delay in completion of work. In the times of automation, any data can be taken from the accounting software or ERP on click of a button, provided the books of account are complete.

The accountants of the company seem to be always so over occupied that there is pendency in their work at all times. Unless you are really understaffed, the accountants/bookkeepers would always keep their tables full of documents and files, that everybody (including themselves) believes that they are the busiest lot in the whole company. Obviously, if they already are so over occupied, how can the management expect another report which is absolutely useless and unnecessary?

As mentioned earlier, if the books of accounts are updated properly by the accountants, pulling out data is not a very hefty task. So, if they say our books are not updated, ask them to do it. After all, that is their KRA (Key Result Area), isn't it?

Actually, the biggest block is in the mind of the management which needs to be cleared. The accountants can easily prepare any report that is required. If one evaluates the work the accountants do in a day, in terms of measurable tasks and approximate turn-around-times for all such tasks, it can be seen that they have enough time to prepare that one more report you are asking for.

Based on our studies of the work profiles of numerous accountants/book-keepers, we found that their planned work constituted only fifty per cent of their day. Rest of their day, they were doing unplanned work which came during the day or week or as a one-time task. Work always expands to fill in the time available, and accountants are no exception. Just closely look into their schedule. You can easily find the time for them to prepare the cash flow that is explained in the subsequent chapters.

Challenge 2

Lack of Will or Determination to review financial statements by the management

Now that we know how to ensure availability of a cash flow statement report made on that basis is available, the next challenge is the unwillingness of the business owner to dig into the details. For that, I have already given the mother-child analogy in the previous chapter. There is nothing more to say on this.

Challenge 3

Accounting cash flows don't tell the true picture

Lastly, the management always feels that the report based on the books of account might not be as per their requirement as there are many things which are recorded as required by the law or accounting principles. So, they feel the report is not as per their understanding of their business, or that it doesn't give the true picture. This challenge is addressed in Chapter *The Management's Cash Flow Statement* where the accounting cash flow statement (prepared based on accounting records) is adjusted to make it a management cash flow statement which is more relevant from the perspective of the management.

Another challenge business owners face is because of the multiple entities that they operate with. In case of large business houses, operations are divided into various proprietorships, partnerships and companies formed at various times keeping in mind, primarily, the family structure of the business owner and obviously, tax planning. The transactions between these entities and with the individuals owning these entities also smudges the cash flow to an extent that one can't make head or tail of what actually happened. The *accounting cash flow statement* can be adjusted for such inter-company transactions while making a *management cash flow statement.* You will get more clarity on this aspect later in this book.

If business owners or the management want to achieve something, nothing can actually stop them. It is only their lethargy and undermining the importance of monitoring their cash flows that comes in the way.

First, at this point, resolve that you shall take immediate action for removing the obstacles you face in monitoring your business more effectively. Then, live your word when the situation demands.

HOW DOES THE FOUR BUCKET CASH FLOW™ HELP?

So, the title of the book and the mention in the previous chapters would have kindled some curiosity in your mind that what exactly is this four bucket cash flow? How does it help the business owner? How different is it from the standard cash flow? What is the tweak?

First, let's understand the Standard Cash Flow Statement which is prepared as per the standard accounting practices. The format of the standard cash flow statement is as under -

	Explanation	Amount (INR)
Cash From Operations (A)	This is the net cash generated as a result of running the main activity of the business. This is calculated by all reducing payments for all expenses (other than interest cost) from the collection on sale/from customers	XXXX
Cash From Financing Activities (B)	This is the derived by reducing cash paid towards loan repayments/interest payments from the cash received as fresh loans	XXXX

Cash From Investing Activities (C)	This is derived by adding cash received from sale of assets/ investments, income earned on investments and reducing any fresh investments or purchase of assets from that total	XXXX
Net Cash Flow (A) + (B) + (C)	The total of 3 cash flows	XXXX

All the inflows and outflows of the money of the business are classified in the above mentioned 3 buckets. The cash flow statement, in this format, gives a lot of clarity and it is an excellent tool to understand how the funds of any business have moved during a period of time. However, in my opinion, and as per my experience, it doesn't give a completely true picture of the movement of funds from the perspective of a small and medium family run business. That is the major reason that the business owners tend to avoid looking at this simple but effective decision-making tool. They only look at their profit and loss statement, and in few cases, also the balance sheet.

The problem arises because of the structuring of capital invested in case of a small business. Many companies (one person or family-owned businesses) operate with bare minimum share capital (say INR One Lac only), and the remaining amount is invested as unsecured loans extended by the family of the business owners. When the movement of these loans is classified as loans along with other loans, the owner is not able to identify how much money they have invested or withdrawn from the business during a period of time.

Further, there are many expenses paid by the business, which are actually personal in nature but booked as business expenditure. Then, there can be certain payments made by the business to the related parties as a part of intelligent tax planning by the consultants or the smart business owners themselves.

All such outflows and inflows blemish the true picture of the cash flows of the business and confuse the business owner.

Hence, I came up with a format which could help smaller businesses to identify how exactly their funds have moved during a period of time.

So, I added a 4th bucket to the cash flow statement to make it more meaningful for the business owner.

The revised format, i.e. the Four Bucket Cash Flow Statement looks as below.

Four Bucket Cash Flow Statement

	Explanation	Amount (INR)
Cash From Operations (A)	This is the net cash generated as a result of running the main activity of the business. This is calculated by all reducing payments for all expenses (other than interest cost) from the collection on sale/from customers	XXXX

Cash From Financing Activities (B)	This is the derived by reducing cash paid towards loan repayments/interest payments from the cash received as fresh loans (except for unsecured loans of the family owners)	XXXX
Cash From Investing Activities (C)	This is derived by adding cash received from sale of assets, income earned on investments and reducing any fresh investments or purchase of assets from that total	XXXX
Cash From Owner's Capital (D)	Fresh amount invested by the owners minus the amounts withdrawn from the business by way of repayment of unsecured loans or payment of expenses to business owners or their related parties	XXXX
Net Cash Flow (A) + (B) + (C) + (D)	The total of 4 Cash Flows	XXXX

This format of the cash flow statement really gives a true picture of the flow of money in the business. It clearly shows that whether the business owners have withdrawn money during a period of time or have they invested money.

You will read in subsequent chapters about how this information is really critical for decision making by business owners. It can change the way they look at their business.

Business owners who have implemented this format and have been consistently reviewing this cash flow statement, have come back and thanked me for giving the much-desired clarity to them as regards to their funds.

.

THE PREREQUISITES – A CHECKLIST

For any report to be meaningful and useful, the underlying data has to be accurate and relevant. As we saw this as a challenge in the earlier chapter also, we know that the cash flow statement has to be prepared from complete and correct data.

To ensure that the accounting data is correct, the accountant has to conform to the management that he has completed certain steps. Or in other words, the management has to ask the accountant if all the required steps had been performed before the data was used for the preparation of the cash flow statement.

The following points are mentioned in a form of a checklist which should be answered before an accountant presents the cash flow statement to the management or the business owner.

S.No.	Task	Done (Y/N)
1.	All bank transactions are recorded and the balance as per books of account and as per bank is reconciled	
2.	All cash transactions are recorded, and cash balance as per books tallies with physical cash in hand	

3.	All purchase and expense invoices are recorded	
4.	All sales invoices raised are booked	
5.	There are no Advance to Creditors for which services have been availed/goods have been received, but only invoice is pending	
6.	There are no pending invoices to be raised against services provided/goods supplied	
7.	There are no suspense entries to be cleared	

The accountant should fill this checklist before he prepares any kind of financial reports, whether it's balance sheet and profit and loss account or the cash flow statement.

Now, the filling of this checklist is very important. Actually, when the management looks at any report prepared by the Finance Department based on accounting data, they assume that the accountant must have ensured all this. The checklist once filled and signed by the accountant relieves the management of all assumptions, and the chances of incorrect analysis and consequent decision making is substantially avoided.

PREPARATION OF THE FOUR BUCKET CASH FLOW STATEMENT

Method 1: Transaction Level Identification

This process of preparation of the four bucket cash flow is very simple and basic. One doesn't need accounting knowledge or experience to understand and even prepare it. Only common sense is required for this exercise, which one has to apply to identify the nature of the payment or receipt so that it can be classified in one of the four buckets.

Here, we just need to understand the Four Buckets of the Cash Flow

Bucket 1 Cash from Operations

Receipts

All receipts from cash sales and collection from debtors, all other receipts related to operations like scrap sale, etc. However, receipts like Interest Income, Dividend, sale of assets and sale of investments are not to be included here.

Payments

The payments towards purchase of materials, all overhead expenses like salaries and wages, staff welfare, electricity, telephone, travel, professional fees, commission and all other operation related payments. However, payments like interest paid, repayment of loan, amount paid to acquire fixed assets, fresh investments made, etc., are not to be included in cash from operations.

Bucket 2 Cash from Financing Activities

Receipts

All receipts from fresh loans from outside the business owner's family. Hence, all fresh term loans from bank, increase in utilisation of bank overdraft and loans taken from non-relatives are included here. The receipts of loans from business owner's family shall be covered in Bucket 4.

Payments

The repayments of loans from outside the business owner's family and the interest payments on such loans shall be included. The repayments of loan to business owner's family and interest payment on such loans shall be covered in Bucket 4.

Bucket 3 Cash from Investing Activities

Receipts

All receipts from sale of assets, sale or maturity of investments, repayments by parties to whom loans were given, interest income, dividend income, etc., form part of the cash inflow from investing activities.

Payments

New assets purchased, fresh investments made, new loans given to parties (other than owner's family or their entities) shall be part of the cash outflow of this bucket.

Bucket 4 Cash from Capital Invested

Receipts

All receipts in form of fresh capital introduced by the business owners and fresh unsecured loans extended by their family are included here.

Payments

All repayments of unsecured loans, capital withdrawn, payments made by the business on behalf of business owners or their family members, etc., are included in the cash outflow of this bucket.

The following steps need to be followed to prepare the cash flow statement, say for a month.

1. List down all the amounts received and payments made from the bank and in cash during the month. For people using any of the commonly used accounting software, this should be readily available as a standard report from the software. The details can be downloaded into MS Excel. All receipts can be taken as positive figures and all payments as negative figures.

2. Once we have the report in MS Excel, we need to write the Bucket (out of the Four Buckets explained above) against each line item, i.e. whether it is a receipt or a payment.

3. After defining buckets for each line item, we need to summarise the report by getting the net flow for each bucket. This can be done using various formulas/tools in MS Excel (like SUMIF formula or PIVOT Table).

4. Once we add the net flow of each bucket to the opening balance of cash in hand/bank balances, the resultant figure should tally with the closing balance of cash in hand/bank balances.

After we are ready with the Four Bucket Cash Flow Statement, we need to do certain other workings and adjustments to the cash flow statement to help us do a better analysis thereof. Those workings are explained in subsequent chapters.

Illustration (figures taken are arbitrary and are taken just for illustrative purposes):

Defining the bucket against each receipt and payment

Item	Amount (Rs.)	Bucket defined
Cash Sales	4,80,000	*Operations*
Machinery Purchased	(2,50,000)	*Investing*
Dividend Income	2,500	*Investing*
Interest Paid	(20,000)	*Financing*
Payment to Suppliers	(8,00,000)	*Operations*
Payment for Expenses	(1,20,000)	*Operations*
Loan Taken from Friend	4,00,000	*Financing*
Increase in Bank OD utilisation	2,50,000	*Financing*
Interest Income on FDR	8,000	*Investing*
Capital introduced by Owner	50,000	*Capital*
Owner's Child's School Fees	(40,000)	*Capital*
FDR Matured	1,00,000	*Investing*
Collection from Customers	1,20,000	*Operations*
LIC Premium Paid	(50,000)	*Capital*

Summary obtained after above classification

Four Bucket Cash Flow Statement

Particulars			Total (Rs.)
Opening Cash/ Bank Balances	A		1,00,000
Add/(Less)			
Cash From Operations	B		
Cash Sales		4,80,000	
Payment to Suppliers		(8,00,000)	
Payment for Expenses		(1,20,000)	
Collection from Customers		1,20,000	(3,20,000)
Financing Activities	C		
Interest Paid		(20,000)	
Loan Taken from Friend		4,00,000	
Increase in Bank OD utilisation		2,50,000	6,30,000
Investing Activities	D		
Machinery Purchased		(2,50,000)	
Dividend Income		2,500	
Interest Income on FDR		8,000	
FDR Matured		1,00,000	(1,39,500)
Owner's Capital	E		
Capital introduced by Owner		50,000	
Owner's Child's School Fees		(40,000)	
LIC Premium Paid		(50,000)	(40,000)
Closing Cash / Bank Balance	F = A + B + C + D + E		2,30,500

Method 2: Cash Flow derived from the Profit and Loss Account and Balance Sheet

In this method, the data is picked up primarily from the other two financial statements, and the cash flow is derived therefrom. For this, a little accounting knowledge might be required. However, the format is more or less the same. Except that, the approach is entirely different.

In Method 1: The analysis is done at transaction level, and cash flow is summarised. There is no pre-requisite that the profit and loss account and balance sheet should be made.

In Method 2? The profit and loss account and balance sheet is prepared first. Then, from these two statements, the cash flow is prepared.

This method was used earlier to prepare the cash flow statement in the Chapter – 'How does the Four Bucket Cash Flow Statement Help?'

Preparation of each bucket is explained below

Bucket 1 Cash from Operations

Here we take the figure of the profit/loss as per profit and loss account and make certain adjustments as under -

	Amount	Remarks
Profit as per Profit and Loss Account	xxx	
Add: Non-Cash items like Depreciation Provisions for Doubtful Debtors/Obsolete Inventory/Warranty, etc. Bad Debts written off	xxx	The non-cash items are added back because they don't lead to any cash outflow, but are reduced while calculating profit.

Add: Interest Paid	xxx	The interest expense is added back as it is considered as cash flow from finance activity
Less: Increase in Current Assets, i.e. Debtors/Stock/ Loans and Advances	xxx	Increase in current assets signifies money not received yet/paid in advance. Hence, it is reduced from profits to derive cash from operations
Add: Decrease in Current Assets, i.e. Debtors/Stock/ Loans and Advances.	xxx	Decrease in current assets signifies money received more than included in profits. Hence, it is added to profits to derive cash from operations
Add: Increase in Current Liabilities, i.e. Creditors/ Expense Payable/Other Liabilities	xxx	Increase in current liabilities signifies payments not made against the expense considered while calculating profit. Hence, it added to profits to derive cash from operations
Less: Decrease in Current Liabilities, i.e. Creditors/ Expense Payable/Other Liabilities	xxx	Decrease in current liabilities signifies more payments made than expense considered while calculating profit. Hence, it is reduced from profits to derive cash from operations
Cash from Operations	xxx	

Bucket 2 Cash from Financing Activities

Here, we take the interest expenditure from the profit and loss account, and the fresh loans received repayments derived are from the difference of opening and closing balances of loans taken.

Bucket 3 Cash from Investing Activities

Here, we take the interest income/dividend income from the profit and loss account (not considered part of the cash from operations). The fresh investments made and proceeds on sale/maturity of investments are derived from the difference of opening and closing balances of various investments made.

Bucket 4 Cash from Owner's Capital Invested

The payments made which pertain to withdrawal of capital are considered whether they are debited to capital account or charged to profit and loss account. The capital invested can be taken from movement in the capital account (or share capital account) and/or the unsecured loans of the owners and their family members.

To explain the method 2 of preparation of a cash flow statement, let me share a real-life case with you. This is about my client, Mr. Vinay Malik, who is an owner of a manufacturing company. One day, he called me and said he was too bogged down by his inability to understand where the money of his business had disappeared. Suddenly, he was in a situation where the business had no funds at all. They had hit a wall it seemed. They didn't know what had gone wrong. Their profit and loss account showed huge profits and their sales was substantially higher than last year. This was clearly an indication that their business was doing very well. Their comparative profit and loss account looked as under -

	Current Year	INR In Crores Previous Year
Sales	30.65	22.78
Less:		
Variable Costs		
(Material, Labour, Factory Electricity etc)	18.40	13.70
	12.25	9.08
Less:		
Fixed Overheads		
(Salaries, Marketing Expenses, Administrative Expenses like Telephone, Office Maintenance, Rent etc.)	5.55	5.23
Profit before Depreciation and Interest	6.70	3.85
Less: Depreciation	0.50	0.60
Less: Interest	1.30	1.00
Net Profit	4.90	2.25
Less: Taxes	1.50	0.65
Profit After Taxes	3.40	1.60

A substantial increase in the net profits over the last year was quite impressive. Then, why was the business short of funds? I asked Vinay, and he was clueless, and rather, furious that the accounts department was not working properly. Had the accounts department been proactive, this situation of no funds would not have arrived.

This set us working on finding out what actually had happened. After having looked at the profit and loss account, now we picked up the balance sheet for scrutiny. We could clearly see from the balance sheet that the debtors had gone up as compared to last year and the stock also was much higher. But, that was obvious; sales had gone up substantially, and hence, debtors and stocks were bound to go up. Since they had higher Cash Credit limits available from the bank now, they had the option of paying creditors early to get huge cash discounts on purchases. So, the creditors actually had not gone up substantially. With huge profits coming in, the company had repaid the loans which would lead to further higher profits available to the owners of the company as the interest cost would substantially go down in the future.

As such, nothing appeared adverse on reading the balance sheet of the company.

The Balance Sheet is shown as below –

		INR in crores
	Current Year	*Previous Year*
Liabilities		
Capital	3.00	3.00
Reserves	6.00	2.60
Loans	1.60	4.00

Current Liabilities		
- Creditors	1.50	1.20
- Bank OD	9.00	5.00
- Provision for Tax	1.50	0.65
	22.60	16.45
Assets		
Fixed Assets	9.00	9.50
Current Assets		
- Debtors	6.85	3.35
- Inventory	6.55	3.50
- Cash and Bank	0.20	0.10
	22.60	16.45

It was clear to us that we can't conclude much from the review of the balance sheet and the profit and loss account. It was clear that to find out the actual movement of funds we will have to prepare a cash flow statement. At first, we made the standard cash flow statement using method 2. The cash flow statement broadly looked like as below –

Standard Cash Flow Statement		*Current Year*
Opening Cash Balance		0.10
Cash Flow from Operations		

Profit after tax	3.40	
Add: Depreciation (non-cash expenditure)	0.50	
Add: Interest (considered as Financing Activity)	1.30	
Less: Increase in Debtors	(3.50)	
Less: Increase in Stock	(3.05)	
Add: Increase in Creditors and Other Liabilities	1.15	(0.20)
Cash Flow from Financing Activities		
Interest Paid	(1.30)	
Bank OD Increased	4.00	
Loans repaid	(2.40)	0.30
Cash Flow from Investing Activities		-

Closing Cash Balance		0.20

From the above, it was so clear that the company had not made any cash from operations even though they had such huge profits during the year. All the money was stuck in the debtors and stock. In order to increase sales, the company was a little liberal on the credit extended to the customers. To avail huge cash discounts on purchases with the additional credit limits available from the bank, they had huge piles of raw material and packing material lying all around the factory. Their credit limit was fully utilised.

But, wait a minute. If the bank had increased the OD limit, why are the cash flows from financing activities so low? So, we can see from the cash flow that the loans have been repaid to the tune of INR 2.40 Crores. On a deeper look, it was found that the loans repaid during the year were actually the unsecured loans of the business owner and his family members. When I confronted Vinay about why had he repaid these loans, he said they withdrew thinking that they were making such huge profits. As the additional working capital was financed by the bank, they thought they can now withdraw their money without impacting the cash flows of the company. Vinay was right to a certain extent, but where he went wrong was that he didn't see if his cash from operations was also positive along with an impressive positive bottom line.

Now, to make my point clear to you, I need to explain this concept first. Here, we see that the unsecured loans extended by Vinay and his family can be called *loans* only for the purpose of accounting. Certainly, that money is more in the nature of capital invested by Vinay in the business and not any *loan*. As mentioned earlier, there are so many companies (family-owned businesses) which operate with bare minimum share capital, of say rupees one lac, and the rest of the capital is invested by the directors and their family as unsecured loans to the company. The obvious reason is the flexibility available for repayment of unsecured loans vis-à-vis the fixed share capital which can't be withdrawn by the shareholders unless at the time of winding up of the company.

When we segregated the loans repaid as Capital Withdrawn and put the repayment as an outflow under the fourth bucket, "Cash from Capital Invested," the cash flow looked as below –

Four Bucket Cash Flow Statement		*Current Year*
Opening Cash Balance		0.10
Cash Flow from Operations		
Profit after tax	3.40	
Add: Depreciation (non-cash expenditure)	0.50	
Add: Interest (considered as Financing Activity)	1.30	
Less: Increase in Debtors	(3.50)	
Less: Increase in Stock	(3.05)	
Add: Increase in Creditors and Other Liabilities	1.15	(0.20)
Cash Flow from Financing Activities		
Interest Paid	(1.30)	
Bank OD Increased	4.00	
		2.70
Cash Flow from Investing Activities		-
Cash Flow from Capital Invested		
Loans Repaid		(2.40)

Closing Cash Balance		0.20

The enhanced OD/CC limit had not only financed the operations, but it had also funded the repayment of loans to the owners of the business, or shall I say, was utilised in withdrawal of their capital invested in the business.

Hence, the four bucket cash flow was born. The standard format of cash flow would always have three buckets – "Cash from Operations," "Cash from Financing Activities" and "Cash from Investing Activities." But, looking at the Indian Scenario and how business owners structure the capital of their companies, it made all the sense to me to add the fourth bucket, i.e. the "Cash from Capital Invested."

Yes, it seems so simple, and the fact is that it is that simple. But, by adding one more bucket in the standard cash flow statement, a much clearer picture emerges for the business owner.

The cash flow statement as per Method 2 can be prepared by accountants easily.

One important point to note here is that even if cash flow statement is made by Method 1 (Transaction level identification), the business owner should ask the accountants to prepare the reconciliation between "Profits" and "Cash from Operations." The reconciling items of these two figures reveal the areas where action might be required to be taken by the business owners. This has been explained in the Chapter, 'Deep Analysis and Action Points.'

In other words, Cash from Operations should be derived from profits using Method 2 separately when the entire cash flow is being made using Method 1.

THE MANAGEMENT'S CASH FLOW STATEMENT

In small and medium enterprises where businesses are run by one person or a few family members, the biggest challenge is the distinction between personal expenses and business expenses. Assets are used commonly for business as well as personal purposes. Many expenses incurred for personal purposes are booked as business expenditure. These practices are not fair, and I am not encouraging them here. It is certainly illegal to charge personal expenses to business. However, if management charges such expenses to the business and sometimes doesn't segregate it, from the perspective of convenience, all that the management is doing, is fooling itself.

The challenge here is that such practices are adopted by the management, and as a result, the financial statements lose their relevance from the management's perspective.

So, when you have charged a lot of personal expenses to the profit and loss account, you tend to mark their payments also under *Bucket 1, i.e. the Cash from Operations*. However, they are actually the withdrawal of capital by the business owners and should be taken to *Bucket 4, i.e. Cash from Capital Invested*.

There can be numerous examples of such expenses where the management can classify them differently based on their understanding. However, the challenge remains that once such expenses are identified, how do we adjust them in the *accountant's cash flow statement* so that one arrives at the *management's cash flow statement?*

For meeting this challenge, we can use the following format to adjust the cash flow statement to make it more meaningful from the management's perspective.

Management's Cash Flow Statement

	Amount	Management adjustment	Relevant Amount
Opening Cash/Bank Balances	100		100
Cash From Operations	600		800
Add: Personal Expenditure debited to Profit and Loss Account		200	
Cash from Financing Activity	(200)		(200)
Cash from Investing Activity	(200)		(200)
Cash from Capital Invested	(100)		(300)
Less: Personal Expenditure (from above)		(200)	
Closing Cash/Bank Balances	200	--	200

If one looks at the above format, the column "management adjustment" can be used by the management to reclassify any payments or receipts as per their understanding and add or subtract any amounts which they want solely for the purpose of their analysis.

Elimination of Inter-Company Transactions

The inter-company transactions in the small and medium-sized businesses really blur the picture, because they unnecessarily hike up the figures, and may create certain illusions in the mind of the business owner.

Let's understand that how elimination of Inter-Company Transactions can bring out the real picture which is more relevant from the perspective of decision making.

For this purpose, let's take a case where there are three companies A, B and C in the ABC Group. A is the manufacturing company, whereas B and C are Trading Companies which market various products (including products of company A) in two different markets respectively.

The Accounting Cash Flow of ABC Group for a year looks like this

Cash Flow (Rs.'ooo)	Company A	Company B	Company C	Total for ABC Group
Operations				
Debtors Collection	4,000	2,500	2,000	8,500
Supplier Payments	(2,000)	(1,800)	(2,700)	(6,500)
Expenses	(300)	(400)	(300)	(1,000)
Total Operations	1,700	300	(1,000)	1,000
Financing				
Loans Taken	500	1,000	1,500	3,000
Loans Repaid	--	(500)	(1,000)	(1,500)
Total Financing	500	500	500	1,500

Investing				
Assets Purchased	(100)	(50)	(75)	(225)
Assets Sold	--	75	--	75
Total Investing	(100)	25	(75)	(150)
Owners' Capital				
Personal Expenses	--	--	(400)	(400)
Total Owner's Capital	--	--	(400)	(400)
Total Cash Flow	2,100	825	(975)	1,950

However, if Inter-Company Transactions are removed from the above cash flow, it might look like:

Cash Flow (Rs.'000)	Company A	Company B	Company C	Total for ABC Group
Operations				
Debtors Collection	4,000	2,500	2,000	8,500
Less: Inter-Company	(4,000)	--	--	(4,000)
Net Collection	--	2,500	2,000	*4,500*
Supplier Payments	(2,000)	(1,800)	(2,700)	(6,500)
Less: Inter Company	--	1,500	2,500	4,000
Net Payment	*(2,000)*	*(300)*	*(200)*	*(2,500)*
Expenses	(300)	(400)	(300)	(1,000)
Total Operations	1,700	300	(1,000)	1,000

Financing				
Loans Taken	500	1,000	1,500	3,000
Less: Inter-Company	(500)	(1,000)	--	(1,500)
Net Loans Taken	--	--	*1,500*	*1,500*
Loans Repaid	--	(500)	(1,000)	(1,500)
Less: Inter-Company	--	500	1,000	1,500
Net Loans Repaid	--	--	--	--
Total Financing	--	--	*1,500*	*1,500*
Investing				
Assets Purchased	(100)	(50)	(75)	(225)
Less: Inter-Company	--	--	75	75
Purchased (Net)	*(100)*	*(50)*	--	*(150)*
Assets Sold	--	75	--	--
Less: Inter-Company	--	(75)	--	--
Sold (Net)	--	--	--	--
Total Investing	*(100)*	*(50)*	--	*(150)*
Owners' Capital				
Personal Expenses	--	--	(400)	(400)
Total Owner's Capital	--	--	*(400)*	*(400)*
Total Cash Flow	1,600	250	100	1,950

Now, let's look at the Cash Flow for ABC Group before and after Inter-Company Transactions:

Cash Flow (Rs.'000)	Before Inter-Company Adjustment	After Inter- Company Adjustment
Operations		
Debtors Collection	8,500	4,500
Supplier Payments	(6,500)	(2,500)
Expenses	(1,000)	(1,000)
Total Operations	1,000	1,000
Financing		
Loans Taken	3,000	1,500
Loans Repaid	(1,500)	--
Total Financing	1,500	1,500
Investing		
Assets Purchased	(225)	(150)
Assets Sold	75	--
Total Investing	(150)	(150)
Owners' Capital		
Personal Expenses	(400)	(400)
Total Owner's Capital	(400)	(400)
Total Cash Flow	1,950	1,950

The analysis of the above management's cash flow statement clearly shows that after adjusting the inter-company transactions, the entire view of the company might change.

Looking at companies individually, B and C had repaid loans totalling to INR 1,500,000. However, at the total group level, no repayments have actually been made. Obviously, the loans taken also are only INR 1,500,000 and not INR 3,000,000.

At the group level, there are no assets sold. Whereas, if we look individually at Company B, there is a cash inflow from sale of assets of INR 75,000.

Further, the collection from debtors from the actual customer is only INR 4,500,000 instead of INR 8,500,000. Now, if this number is compared to the Sales Figure (net of Inter-company transactions), one can get to know what percentage is still outstanding. Inter-company transactions in any business, blur the true view of the business. They should be ignored for any kind of analysis, and the way to tackle them is well-explained above.

PROJECTED CASH FLOWS AND MONITORING ACTUALS

Making financial projections is only a theatrical exercise for most of the business owners. They think of projected financial statements as nothing more than a requirement by the bank for revising the Overdraft or Cash Credit Limit. Such financial projections are prepared by the accountants of the company along with support from the chartered accountant firm, primarily from the bank's perspective.

In most of the cases, the business owners never make the projected financial position of their businesses for the purpose of monitoring their growth and profitability. Even though everyone has a target in mind in relation to the sales figure for the year and even for the profit they wish to earn, business owners would never be comfortable preparing a detailed projected balance sheet and profit and loss account, and then, review their actual performance against the balance sheet and account. The biggest question in their mind is that how could they tell in advance how much they will be able to sell during the year. Then, don't all the expenses depend on the level of operations? If making projections for profits and sales is so difficult, the preparation of a projected cash flow statement certainly is a far cry from achievable.

However, if an effort is made with a few assumptions around credit available to the company from its' debtors and credit allowed to the creditors, then the company can certainly make a projected cash flow statement. Obviously, a lot of other assumptions like growth in sales, expenses and profits plan for capital expenditure, etc., also have to be considered while making the projected cash flow.

In other words, the projected inflows can be predicted based on the projected monthly sales and average credit period extended to the customers. Similarly, the projected outflows can be predicted based on the projected purchases, expenses and the credit period available from vendors.

The projected loan repayments can be taken from the loan repayment schedules. The interest payments on overdrafts can be estimated based on the projected levels of utilisation of overdraft limits, again, as per the projected balance sheets. The payments for acquiring assets can also be taken from the projected balance sheets for the purpose of projected cash flow statement.

The biggest challenge in making projections is that people think that the actuals are going to be different, and the purpose of preparing a projected cash flow statement is going to be a futile exercise. And, as they say, 'The start is the biggest stop.' They don't even try once.

I suggest one should start by attempting the projected financial statements (including the projected four bucket cash flow statement) for each month. Make mistakes in projecting, keep learning and correcting yourself as you review and revise your monthly projections.

A high level projected cash flow statement might look like this (i.e. once the actuals are captured against the projections) -

	Planned for the month (Rs.'ooo)	Actual for the month (Rs.'ooo)	Difference (Actual minus Planned)
Opening Cash/Bank Balances	100	100	--
Cash From Operations	600	500	(100)
Cash from Financing Activity	(200)	(200)	NIL
Cash from Investing Activity	(200)	(300)	(100)
Cash from Capital Invested	(100)	--	100
Closing Cash/Bank Balances	200	100	(100)

However, the beauty lies in the details. If you really wish to make a very effective projected four bucket cash flow statement, I suggest that you make the projections as detailed as possible (and later actuals captured accordingly). The projections and actuals can look as below -

	Planned for the month (Rs.'000)	Actual for the month (Rs.'000)	Difference (Actual minus Planned)
Cash From Operations			
Cash Sales	500	550	(50)
Collection from Customers	400	275	(125)
M/s Customer 1	350	325	(25)
M/s Customer 2	250	250	(0)
M/s Customer 3			
Total Collection	1500	1300	(200)
Payments to Suppliers			
M/s Supplier 1	200	180	(20)
M/s Supplier 2	100	70	(30)
M/s Supplier 3	150	140	(10)
M/s Supplier 4	150	110	(40)
Payment for Expenses			
Telephone Expenses	10	9	(1)
Electricity Expenses	20	16	(4)
Rent	55	55	--
Salaries	210	210	--
Office Expenses	5	10	5
Total Payments	900	800	(100)
Net Cash from Operations	600	500	(100)

Further, for projecting payments for specific expenses, one needs to go further deep into details. Say, for telephone expenses, one can make the projections telephone number wise and then capture actual expenditure as shown below –

	Planned for the month (Rs.'000)	Actual for the month (Rs.'000)	Difference (Actual minus Planned)
Telephone Expenses			
Mob No. 99999XXXXX	1	2	1
Mob No. 99111XXXXX	1	3	2
Mob No. 98888XXXXX	2	2	--
Landline No. 4610XXXX	3	1	(2)
Landline No. 4610XXXX	3	1	(2)
Total	10	9	(1)

If one prepares details like the above for each head of expenditure, the projections can be pretty accurate and much relevant for the purpose of monitoring actuals against them.

The details should be well documented and looked into very carefully by the management. It is possible that at the total level for a particular head of expense, the deviation of actuals from the projections, might not appear substantial or relevant. But, a deeper look into the details can actually reveal facts which can be relevant from the management's perspective and may call for an action to be taken.

Say for example, in the telephone expenses, as shown above, we can say that anybody would ignore a deviation of INR 1,000 in totality as it is only 5% of the total amount paid. However, on the analysis of the detail, it clearly shows that the deviation in couple of mobile phone cases is huge and should be looked into by the business owner for understanding if any deduction is to be made on account of personal calls made by the user of the telephone. The increase in mobile phone bills though got compensated by lesser landline usage. So, we can say that one has to dig down deep to find the real reasons by breaking down expenses to the lowest levels possible.

I understand that I have taken the case of telephone expenses which is relatively a very simple example. If we would have taken a complex head of account like repair and maintenance of machinery, it would have been a little difficult to explain the concept. However, in such cases, you can always prepare the projections based on certain assumptions which can be drawn based on the actual data of the previous months or years.

Planning of personal withdrawal from the business

The projected four bucket cash flow statement can effectively help you plan your withdrawals from the business so that you can take care of your personal finance as well. Further, it can help you identify the need for temporary funding from outside sources, much well in advance so that there are no last minute surprises.

This is particularly relevant in case of businesses of seasonal nature. Let us take example of an educational institution which collects the fee from its students only twice in a year, i.e. April (1st Semester) and October (2nd Semester). You know that the collections will come in April and October every year. So, you can plan your own withdrawals accordingly and plan your personal expenditure accordingly. Further, one would see from this projected cash flow statement that the surplus cash generated in the business season shall be required to finance the expenses to be incurred in the non-season months. Hence, temporary short term investments can be planned with maturity-time matching with the non-cash generating time of the year. The typical cash flow of the above educational institution for a quarter, say April to June every year, will look as below.

	April (Rs.'000)	May (Rs.'000)	June (Rs.'000)
Opening Cash/Bank Balances	100	100	100
Cash From Operations			
Fees Collected	2400		
Less: Monthly Expenditure	(180)	(180)	(180)
Cash from Financing Activity	--	--	--
Cash from Investing Activity			
Invested in short term Fixed Deposits	(2200)	--	--
Maturity of 1-month Fixed Deposit	--	200	--
Maturity of 2 months Fixed Deposit	--	--	200
Cash from Capital Invested	(20)	(20)	(20)
Closing Cash/Bank Balances	100	100	100

By realising that the funds will be needed every month for expenses, the business owner running this educational institution doesn't immediately withdraw large amount of money in April (even if collected) and invests the collected amount in short term investments to fund the monthly expenses. They also plan their own money withdrawals on a monthly basis accordingly keeping in mind the monthly money saved from operations. Such practices lead to a high degree of discipline in running of the business.

DEEP ANALYSIS AND ACTION POINTS

What is the use of the food which is not consumed and goes into the dustbin? Similarly, what is the use of a report which is not analysed and goes into the shredder?

The first challenge is to make the accountant prepare the additional report called the Four Bucket Cash Flow Statement. The accountant may feel that this report is actually not needed by the business owner. His feeling is confirmed once he sees that the report he prepared sitting after office hours has not been even looked at by you. He will not prepare it the next month for sure.

If you as a business owner have realised what a four bucket cash flow can tell you, please allow it to tell you the same. Now, this will happen only when you sit across the table with your four bucket cash flow statement and let it pour its heart out in front of you.

On a serious note, only by devoting a certain amount of time and energy in the analysis of any financial statement, can you understand what exactly it is indicating. At first, you may not be able to notice all the relevant points. But, consistent and persistent reviews can help you master the skill of picking up the relevant action points with ease.

Now, let us understand what you can analyse from a four bucket cash flow statement.

Reasons for low cash from operations

The reconciliation of cash flow statement and the profit and loss account (as discussed earlier) can be used to identify the places where the business' cash is stuck. Now, suppose the cash from operations are lower than the net profits, we get to know that the reason is that the inventories have gone up during the month. A closer review should be done of the inventories ageing with a specific inquiry of items which are slow-moving or becoming non-moving. Maybe, the management has to take a decision to off-load those items timely and free-up their cash. Whatever decision is taken, it will be at least a conscious one based on analysis of some information.

Another very obvious reason for low cash from operations can be lower profits than projected profits. In that case, the reasons for lower net profits have to be looked into. Again, when an in-depth analysis is done, one may stumble upon expenses which have gone beyond acceptable limits. The reasons should be thoroughly examined, and necessary action be taken immediately. This has been discussed in detail in the chapter, *'Take Specific Action – SEDUCE.'*

Application of loan funds

If long term funds are applied to short term use, it is not an alarming situation, because it does not affect the liquidity of the business. But, in case short term funds are applied for long term purposes, it can be fatal for the enterprise. Obviously, the liability of a short-term loan will become due earlier than the realisation of the long term asset.

So, if the second bucket shows that the utilisation of Cash Credit limit has gone up, and at the same time the third bucket shows money paid for purchasing machinery, you need to look into it immediately. Maybe, you have to take a term loan for the machinery and ensure that Cash Credit limit is available for short term needs of the business.

Monitoring Capital withdrawals

I have seen four bucket cash flow statements which showed that the withdrawal of funds for personal use had been made by the business owners even when cash generated from operations was negative. That meant that the withdrawals were made from either loan funds or amounts received on sale of assets or investments.

The source of funds that have been withdrawn by the business owner during the month should be known to them in any case. This analysis can lead to an action to being taken, like returning the money to the business.

The key to analysis is to identify specific actions which should be taken to ensure that the liquidity of the business is either restored or maintained. In this case, the cash from operations.

TAKE SPECIFIC ACTIONS - SEDUCE

As explained in the earlier chapter that on analysis of the gap between the "net profit as per profit and loss account" and "cash from operations," one can find out where are the areas where money is stuck, and we will find that it is majorly two, i.e. Stocks and Debtors.

Furthermore, if the *net profit* is lower, then it is obvious that the *cash from operations* is going to be low. One way to increase net profit is to increase margins. Sometimes, this becomes a challenge in a competitive market. Then, the only way to increase the profitability is to cut down costs. Again, as per my experience in dealing with clients, I have noticed that the when expenses go up with increase in business, sometimes, they increase disproportionately. On periodic intervals, depending on case to case, one has to go back and look at the expenses to see where the wasteful expenditure is and how it could be saved.

In view of what has been discussed above, it can be said that the key to have a comfortable cash flow position is to keep the Stock, the Debtors and Expenses in check at all times and at all levels of business. This has to be a continuous process.

To make people remember this critical action of reviewing and controlling the above elements, I use the word SEDUCE which stands for:

Stock

Expenses

Debtors

Under

Control

Eternally

The above acronym, if taken in the right spirit and applied in your business, can pull your business out of the cash crunch situations, and will never let you slip into one again.

That will not only make the cash flow position of the company better, but it will also substantially increase the profitability and sustainability of your business.

Now, let's take each element, i.e. Stock, Expenses and Debtors separately, and see what specific actions can be taken to keep the three in check.

The entire book, until now, has just spoken about the four bucket cash flow statement. However, the actions that you are going to read now can be taken even if the cash flow statement is not made by the business owner. The Four Bucket Cash Flow Statement is an indicator which leads us to take these actions. You can get these indicators from other means also, including your gut feeling.

Let's look at each element and proposed actions now.

STOCK

All the following steps help keep the inventory at optimum levels and avoid cash getting trapped in the form of inventory.

1. *Proper Stacking of material or goods*

It is such a basic task which should be done in any case, i.e. whether you have higher stocks or not. If the stocks are properly stacked and are easily visible, the chances of you they getting used or sold is higher. I have seen cases where the material was already there lying in the store, but fresh purchases were made to supply customers. This happens when stock is not stored systematically. Even if the store records show that the material is in stock, it is not found physically due to improper storage.

The use of racks and bins for smaller items and marked separate isles on floor for heavier goods, make the storage more organised.

If you haven't done it for a long time, just stack your stock properly, and you can be surprised what you have in store and what you don't have.

All assumptions around your stock just go out of the window if it is properly stacked and can be identified and retrieved conveniently. However, you get to know this only when you do it.

2. *Physical Verification and Reconciliation*

The periodic physical verification of inventory highlights the shortages, excesses and breakages of material. It should preferably be done by an external agency. If done internally, it should be done by non-operations team members.

The stock should first be counted physically and then compared to inventory records to highlight shortages and excesses. The reasons for the differences should be obtained and analysed by the business owner.

3. *Store Records have to be maintained*

In my interaction with business owners, I realised that, in certain cases, strict physical security control was kept on the movement of goods inward and outward of the premises. In such cases, the inventory records were not maintained properly. The business owners claimed that their physical controls ensure that no theft or pilferage takes place.

Hence, they never appreciated the importance of maintaining proper stock records. I fail to understand that if no proper records are maintained, how they could know how much stock is there in the premises at any point of time. Such a lack of information also affects the purchase decisions and ability to recognise theft or pilferage.

4. *Inventory Management System*

A proper Inventory Management System should be put in place. For this purpose, ideally, a software-based solution should be used. However, where volumes are less, a basic MS Excel sheet can also serve the purpose. How much technology is to be deployed depends on the scale and nature of business.

Whatever tool is used to maintain inventory, the purpose is to have an effective control over the stock so that there is never excess nor shortage of any item. The same can be achieved through defining maximum levels and reorder levels of all the stock items. If all the stock items seem difficult, start with top twenty per cent items. A real-time updating of receipt and issue of material in the stock records should be upheld to make it an effective system.

5. Don't order in Bulk for Discounts

A common mistake committed by businesses is that they overbuy inventory just because it seems profitable. The fact is that whatever we overbuy, sometimes remain unsold for a long time. Often, such excess stocks bought in greed of a little more discounts are disposed-off at rates much lower than anticipated. Further, the carrying costs of this stock add to the loss incurred. For most businesses, it is any day better to follow just-in-time inventory.

6. Analyse Ageing of Stock

Inventory records should be capable of conveniently providing information of slow-moving and non-moving stocks. A policy should be put in place which defines the action that needs to be taken to dispose-off the inventory which crosses a defined age in the system. Periodic reviews of inventory should be done. You must also ensure that the appropriate actions are taken in a timely manner as per the policy.

7. Identifying alternate use of old stock

Once old stock is identified, alternate uses should be identified wherein major savings can be achieved if the non-moving stock can be used in place of new stock with some amendments involving minimal cost.

8. Make the Store Rooms smaller, if possible

The excess space earmarked for keeping stock becomes a reason why no action is taken for timely disposing-off of the non-moving inventory.

To highlight such old stock, a separate area should be defined in the premises, and these items should be moved from the main stores to this "Non-Moving" store.

The purpose of having a separate area is that the non-moving items don't mix with the fast moving ones. The physical view of such an inventory is a trigger for action. The record of such stocks alone might not have the same impact.

EXPENSES

1. Monitoring the Trend of Expenses

The expenses generally follow a pattern. Either, they are fixed, or they are variable. Based on the nature of expenses, the movement of these expenses from month to month should be evaluated.

The expenses which should increase or decrease in direct proportion to the level of activity should always move in the appropriate direction. If they don't change in line with the change in related activity, then the reasons should be looked into. Often, factors leading to pilferage or wastage are unearthed on such analysis.

In most of the cases, an off-the-trend item indicates an action that should be taken. However, a constant outflow in a certain head also might indicate some leakages. That is when a variable expense doesn't vary with the change in level of activity.

Let's understand this with help of an example. Look at the following chart with expenses at different levels of production.

	Apr	May	Jun	Jul	Aug	Sep
Production (in Units)	3,000	4,000	4,500	3,500	2,500	3,000
Expense (in Rs.'000)						
Raw Material	6,000	8,000	9,000	7,000	5,000	6,000
Fuel Expenses	600	900	1,200	1,000	1,000	1,200
Labour	2,500	2,500	2,500	2,500	2,500	2,500
Electricity	1,500	1,900	2,200	1,800	1,400	1,500

On analysis of the above expenses, we observe -

Raw Material

The consumption of Raw Materials is in line with the level of production activity, and it is consistent over the months. Hence, there is nothing to raise the eyebrows of the management.

Fuel Expenses

The expenses rise with increase in level of production activity from April to June, which seems alright. However, the fuel expenses didn't come down proportionately in the drop in activity in the month of July. Further, it doesn't drop and stays pretty high in subsequent months irrespective of the level of activity. On analysis of the reasons, it can be found that there is a drop in efficiency of the generators due to delay in its periodic servicing. Immediate action of getting the generators serviced can restore its efficiency, and fuel costs can be brought back to normal levels.

Labour

Strangely, Labour expenses are fixed at INR 2,500,000 every month. It doesn't change whether the business produces 4,500 or it produces 2,500. As a possible remedial action, the fixed labour force can be curtailed, and more contractual labour should be taken. Or, an alternate piece rate system can be adopted instead of fixed wages.

Electricity

The electricity expenses are moving more or less in line with the production activity. Hence, no action is required to be taken on this front.

2. Budgeting and Monitoring – Deep Level

The best way to exercise control over fixed expenses is to create budgets and monitor the actual expenses against the set budgeted amounts.

For a budget to be effective, it should be built from bottom-up. That means, defining budgets for smallest possible item of expense, and then, clubbing them into relevant heads of expenses. Say, for instance, individual budgets can be allocated for each mobile connection being used in the company. Then, all these individual mobile phone budgets can be added to get the total budget for Mobile Expenses.

While analysing, the comparison of actuals to budget should also be done at the individual mobile number level, and then on a total basis. The correct action will be identified only when analysis is done at the deepest level, and not on the overall level.

3. CRE Analysis

CRE stands for Continue, Reduce or Eliminate.

CRE analysis of expenses should be done at periodic intervals. For doing this analysis, inputs should be taken from the end users, i.e. those members of the team who cause the expenses.

The purpose is to evaluate whether any expenses have to continue as it is, or some changes can be made to reduce them, or could they be completely eliminated.

The following is an illustration of CRE analysis

Head of Account	Amount (INR)	CRE Action
Salaries and Wages	1,500,000	Reduce
Digital Marketing	50,000	Continue
Hoarding Advertisement	500,000	Eliminate
Fax Machine AMC	1,500	Eliminate
Water Filter AMC	1,500	Continue
Telephone Expenses	25,000	Reduce
Electricity Expenses	100,000	Reduce
Business Promotion	25,000	Reduce
Truck Running Expenses	50,000	Reduce
Security and Housekeeping	50,000	Continue

4. Mindful Resource Management

All businesses experience phases of growth and decline. When there is a decline phase, at that time the management might become alert and cut down costs to save themselves. However, the real challenge is to apply resources when the business is growing mindfully.

When everything is happening in their favour and business increases, either steadily or there are sudden spurts of growth, the business owners tend to go on a hiring spree and add people to various departments. In fact, with increase in volume of the business, certain departments which were not there earlier come into existence. However, in the celebration of the sales turnover touching new heights, the businesses ignore the inefficiencies that creep into the system.

To keep a check on the cost of resources and to ensure the efficiencies in their performance, we can apply certain tools which are discussed here. The practical implementation of these tools requires a significant effort and discipline. Since the effort is in the present and the results are in the future, people might give up applying these tools after a few days of trial. However, it has to be understood, accepted and practised that for any action to be effective; it has to be performed consistently and persistently.

i. Timesheet

This tool is so simple yet so effective for resource management. In service industries, where billing is done based on time spent on client servicing, timesheets are filled by all operational staff, and that makes absolute sense to everyone.

However, the concept of timesheets being filled by the administrative staff of a manufacturing organisation might not appear to be of any value to many.

The timesheet shows the mirror. It clearly summarises what one is doing the entire day. When that data is captured by the people themselves, the realisation of how much time is being wasted looks straight into their faces.

Believe me, if the business owners themselves fill their own timesheets, they will realise how much time they waste in a day. I am telling you this from experience. The moment you become conscious of where your time is going, and you are documenting time, it does magic to your efficiencies.

Just make people note what they do every hour of the day. Initially, tell them to do that for a week. Obtain those records of work done by them in that one week. The inefficiencies will be jumping out those timesheets like you see dolphins jump out of the water in a dolphin show. It is a spectacular view. One thing is for sure, and it is that you will clearly see a resistance to fill the time sheet by your people. You have to decide for yourself whether you wish to continue making them fill or use it as a tool at periodic intervals or when you see any individual derailing from the track.

ii. **Organisation Chart**

In most of the cases, business owners don't make organisation charts for their businesses because they know their businesses like the back of their hands. In their minds, there is no need to put it on paper and then to analyse it. They can go around their establishments and physically see who is doing what and that according to them is more effective than putting it in the form of a document.

However, organisation charts should made in detail with clearly defined roles and responsibilities along with the details of the number of people in each role, irrespective of the size of the businesses. I am not elaborating on what is an organisation chart. One can search the internet to get enough information about it.

The Organisation Chart gives you a bird's eye view of your business. The review with following intentions might provide the respective action points described here.

Intention of Review	Possible Action Point
Find out possible areas of duplication of effort	Roles and responsibilities redefined Movement of people within departments
Find out jobs which can be combined	Consolidating similar work done by various departments and by putting in place a separate support function.
Rearranging the reporting structure	Movement of people within departments or introduce cross-functional reporting to align efforts of all towards a common goal
Identifying redundant functions	To abandon certain activities which are no longer required
Finding missing links or important vacant positions	To hire people, or to move from other departments to fill the gap
Identifying overstaffing in any of the departments	To optimise the number of people by laying off or moving to other departments
Identify areas being managed by the business owner themselves which might require delegation and accordingly resources need to be hired or allocated for the same	To hire people or move them from other departments to manage a department or task

iii. **Work Management**

The work to be performed, if well defined in advance, can be a guide to people performing the tasks. One way is to work on what requires immediate action and ensure that it is completed on time. The other way is to plan everything, document it and ensure that it is performed accordingly.

Core Operations

A plan for what is to be produced on a daily basis can be prepared based on average efficiencies and capacities. This plan is to be prepared by a senior and given to the doer of the task.

iv. **Chasers for Follow Up**

When the production is planned, one should appoint chasers who maintain a strong follow up with the doers to ensure they achieve the planned output for the day.

The chasers should not only chase for performance, but they should also act instrumental in getting all hurdles removed and problems solved for the doers by escalating the same with the relevant managers.

The chasers should ensure that the actual production or work done is recorded so that a meaningful and timely comparison of plan and actual can be done. This data can also help in measuring the performance which is explained in the next point.

v. **Performance Measurement**

If the key results expected of any function or team member is well defined and in measurable terms, then the data around the actual performance on that parameter can be captured easily.

So, the first task is to define the key results expected from a particular person. Then, a system should be put in place to capture information around the performance of that task on a regular basis. The actual performance data captured should be placed against the expected Key Result, and the person's performance should be evaluated accordingly on a regular basis, say weekly or monthly.

Suppose the key result from a tele-caller is to generate 100 leads every month, the actual number of leads generated by her during the month should be noted and compared to 100 leads to see how much result she has achieved during the month.

This performance evaluation system has to be put in place for each individual in the company. Just that Key Result Areas need to be defined for each person, and a system to capture information should be put in place.

The data, when available for a long period of time, say a year, tells you a lot about a person's performance. This can also help the person keep a track of how behind they are from achieving the expected results.

5. Better Vendor Management

The Vendors are the lifelines of any business. If they don't do what they do, their customers will not be able to do business. However, the customer being a more powerful person always tries to take maximum advantage from the vendor. The biggest advantage a customer seeks, more than a great price, is the credit period one can take from the supplier.

However, as far as I am aware, no vendor leaves the opportunity of a higher price if the credit period is longer.

The vendor might build in an interest component in the price which might be much higher than the bank's rate of interest.

The interest component is evident from the cash discount a vendor offers. The discount might range between 2% to 10% on advance or down payment. An informed and well-calculated decision should be taken, i.e. whether to avail credit period or avail cash discount. Do whatever maximises the profit.

Further, in case a company consistently delays payments to vendors, it loses all the power to negotiate. However, if you pay your vendors promptly and on the promised dates, the vendors also treat the company nicely, and keep their dealings fair.

Nobody likes to work with poor paymasters. Become your vendor's favourite customer.

6. Wastages

This is one area which eats up profits like a termite. If proper preventive treatment is not done, this silent killer can cause serious damages.

The companies which define maximum permissible wastages in operations and then take immediate remedial action when the water goes above the danger mark are the ones maintaining consistently higher gross margins in the industry.

The problem with wastages is that if they become the norm, then no one will ever do anything to curb them.

The best way to control is to measure them. Record the wastages, calculate the averages, set the standards, monitor against the standards and take immediate action on noting deviations.

If the wastages are consistently lower than the standards, then revise the standards to the new lower level.

However, if it even for once goes higher than the standard, get into the reason and eliminate possibilities of that event recurring in the future.

7. Lower the Interest Cost

Interest Costs eat up profits like no other expense item does.

Electricity is not spent if the office is not working or when the factory has the weekly off. However, the interest charge will still be levied by the lender for that day. Interest is charged even the national holidays or the festivals. It just never stops, until the time you repay the loan.

However, by intelligent and timely working on alternate sources of funds or shifting credit facilities to other banks, one can substantially reduce the interest costs.

The loyalty towards your old nationalised bank might be costing you a hella lot of money. Explore other products and services available which might bring down the interest costs.

When you explore others, your old bankers suddenly become willing to reduce the interest rates and other charges.

Needless to say that when it comes to pre-payment of loans, finish of the high-interest loans first.

DEBTORS

1. Analyse Payment Performance

The payment performance of each customer should be evaluated, i.e. how much time do they take to pay each invoice. The average number of days in which payments are made by customers for each invoice would reveal their true payment performance.

Generally, we have an overall feeling that whether a client pays on time or not. However, the invoice-wise number of days' collection would clearly establish basis for our feeling. Then, it is a fact-based opinion and not a general feeling.

If a customer's average days are more than the other, we clearly know whom we should deal with. Further, the larger customers end up taking advantage of the suppliers' dependence on them, and their payments become slower over a period of time. Business owners also easily ignore the delay for large customers.

With a regular review of the customers' performance, a business owner can become alert the moment he/she sees a downward trend.

The choice can be made in time whether to continue supplying goods and services to such defaulting customers.

2. Consider Interest Cost and Decide

If the number of days' collection and amount outstanding against each invoice are available, one can calculate the interest borne by the business because the customer didn't pay on time. Such interest costs should be reduced from the profit earned from such customers to arrive at the real profit of dealing with that customer.

It may come out that the amount earned from larger customers turns out to be lower than the smaller ones because of lower margins and higher interest costs.

When you look at the comparison of the profits earned (net of interest costs) vis-a-vis the sales to various customers, it can again help taking a well-informed decision whether to continue business with any customer or not.

Illustration –

Customer	Sales	Profit earned	Interest cost on average outstanding	Real Profit earned	% earned
A	10,000	2,000	NIL	2,000	20%
B	20,000	3,800	600	3,200	16%
C	30,000	5,400	2,400	3,000	10%
D	40,000	7,000	1,000	6,000	15%

One can clearly see that dealing with C is not that profitable as compared to other customers. Either C mends his way or one looks for an alternate customer and discontinues supplies to him.

3. Ageing of Debtors

Another way to monitor the customers' outstanding amounts is by their ageing. The moment one sees overdue amounts in the ageing, one can immediately initiate action on collection of the overdue invoices. This can lead to faster collection and lower the interest costs of the business.

An illustration of debtors ageing is as below –

	Number of days outstanding				
Customer	0–30	30–60	60–90	90–180	Above 180
A	3,000	1,500	–	–	–
B	2,800	3,000	1,500	700	500
C	2,500	2,000	1,500	1,000	–
D	3,000	–	–	–	–

In the above illustration, it is evident that the customers can be easily rated from highest to lowest in their payment performance as D, A,C and then B.

If one sees a customer moving from "lesser number of days" bracket to "more number of days" bracket, one should become alert and decide whether to supply more to the customer or not.

4. The Credit Control

Large corporations set the credit limits for customers based on their analysis of the customer. They might look at various factors and decide how much credit is to be extended to each customer.

No matter what happens, salespeople are not allowed to sell if the credit limit of the customer has been reached. Credit limits can be revised, but with approvals from the top management, and credit limits have to be justified before approval.

However, smaller businesses get excited and start extending credit to their customers without evaluating their credit-worthiness. This way, they expose themselves to huge risks every day without even realising. They fund even those customers whom the banks are also not willing to fund.

It is really difficult to let go of a sale, and hence, they succumb to the pressure and extend more credit to the already defaulting customer.

Sometimes, such risks taken lead to actual loss; i.e. the debtors becoming bad and the amount becoming irrecoverable.

Business owners should be extra cautious with credit limits extended, and they should also ensure that they adhere to these limits and abstain from selling to customers if the amount outstanding is crossing the set credit limit.

5. Collection System

A formal collection system should be put in place wherein a collection coordinator should be dedicated for following up with the customers.

Generally, business owners follow up for payment themselves, or they ask their accounts team to follow up. In certain cases, the follow up for collection is done by the sales team. Neither of these people can be really effective in collecting money from the customers.

The collection coordinator should make regular phone calls, send emails and messages and keep track of the due dates or committed dates for payment. A regular follow up by a coordinator brings better results than anyone else doing the follow-up with customers.

S.E.D.U.C.E.

The above actions can be taken up one by one, which will make your cash flow position far better than it ever was. This will make your company a cash-rich one with reserves which you can utilise for expansion of your business and lead a great personal life.

FOLLOW-THROUGH

A follow-through is something that completes an action or a planned series of actions. In other words, if you follow through an action, plan, or an idea (or follow through with it), you continue doing or thinking about it until you have done everything possible.

Like in the game of golf, what decides the quality of a shot is the follow through, i.e. the part of the stroke after the ball has been hit.

In context of the four bucket cash flow statement, the mere preparation of the statement, the adjustments done to make it a management cash flow statement, the deep analysis and taking note of the action points, all become meaningless, if a proper follow-through is missing.

Hence, the business owner has to review and revisit the actions that were identified as part of the analysis done by him. Obviously, most of the tasks or actions are to be performed by the team members of this business owner and not himself. If he is poor at keeping a track of the follow-ups, then all that he does will be highly ineffective.

Hence, a proper system should be in place to monitor the actions to be taken. A format of a table where such information can be captured is given below –

Action Items Identified	Person Responsible	Target Date for Corrective Action	Actual Date of Action Taken	Details of action taken
Increase in Debtors (Average no. of days up to 120 from 90 days)	Sales Head	18-May	20-May	Credit terms enforced effectively
Increase in Inventory	Plant Head (with Stores In Charge)	25-May	Still Pending	Get rid of non-moving Stock
Short Term Funds utilised for Long Term purposes	CFO and Business Owner	5-May	10-May	Term Loan taken from bank
Excess drawings by Business Owner	Business Owner	31-May	31-May	Rationalising drawings in line with cash position

All actions should have a completion date, and the business owner should follow up adequately to ensure that the people responsible for completion of the task do it by that date. If they are not able to do it by the designated date for any reason, they should finish it within a reasonable time. A proper follow-through will ensure that whatever is required is actually accomplished.

The four bucket cash flow gives enough information to business owners to manage their businesses effectively, and if they master the science of this cash flow statement, their getting into a financial mess is nearly impossible. Go ahead, take a step today towards making your four bucket cash flow statement - a report that you will review for the rest of your life.

Manufactured by Amazon.ca
Bolton, ON